D0936718

OBESITY

OBESITY

Terry Allan Hicks

 **Marshall Cavendish**
Benchmark
New York

For Jack, who shows me every day how to lead a healthier life

Special thanks to Carolyn Bradner Jasik, MD, Division of Adolescent Medicine, University of California, San Francisco, for her expert review of the manuscript.

Marshall Cavendish Benchmark
99 White Plains Road
Tarrytown, New York 10591-5502
www.marshallcavendish.us

This book is not intended for use as a substitute for advice, consultation, or treatment by a licensed medical practitioner. The reader is advised that no action of a medical nature should be taken without consultation with a licensed medical practitioner, including action that may seem to be indicated by the contents of this work, since individual circumstances vary and medical standards, knowledge, and practices change with time. The publisher, author, and medical consultants disclaim all liability and cannot be held responsible for any problems that may arise from use of this book.

Library of Congress Cataloging-in-Publication Data

Hicks, Terry Allan.
Obesity / by Terry Allan Hicks.
p. cm. — (Health alert)
Summary: "Provides comprehensive information on the causes, treatment, and history of obesity"—Provided by publisher.
Includes index.
ISBN 978-0-7614-2911-1
1. Obesity—Juvenile literature. I. Title.
RC628.H487 2009
616.3'98—dc22
                    2007031246

Front cover: A model of part of the hormone peptide YY, which helps regulate appetite
Title page: Another model view of the hormone peptide YY

Photo Research by Candlepants Incorporated

Cover Photo: Alfred Pasieka / Photo Researchers Inc.

The photographs in this book are used by permission and through the courtesy of:
Photo Researchers Inc.: Alfred Pasieka, 3 ; David M. Phillips, 5; Phanie, 9; Gusto, 13; Josh Sher, 51. *Corbis*: Jennie Woodcock; Reflections Photolibrary, 7; Karen Kasmauski, 11, 24, 54; Pat Doyle, 20; Michael A. Keller/zefa, 22; Forestier Yves/SYGMA, 26; Araldo de Luca, 32; Bettmann, 35; Ashley Cooper, 39; Poisson d'Avril/Photocuisine, 40; CHIP EAST/Reuters, 47; Mark Richards, 52, 53. *The Image Works*: Michael Siluk, 15. *Getty Images*: Werner Blessing, 16; Donna Day, 30. *Index Stock*: Steve Dunwell, 17. *Super Stock*: age fotostock, 29. *USDA.gov*: 38, 55. *Alamy Images*: Tom Mareschal, 41. *Digital Railroad*: Ambient Images, 43. *PhotoTakeUSA.com*: BSIP, 45, 48, 50.Photo research by Candlepants, Inc.

Editor: Joy Bean
Publisher: Michelle Bisson
Art Director: Anahid Hamparian

Printed in Malaysia
6 5 4 3 2 1

CONTENTS

WHAT IS IT LIKE TO BE OBESE?

Every day, all across America, you can see children enjoying physical **exercise**. Whether they are practicing shots on a basketball court, skipping rope on a school playground, or just running around in a city park, they are getting the pleasure and good health benefits that come from moving their bodies. But you can also see children—far too many of them—who cannot join in these activities, because they suffer from a serious medical condition called **obesity**, caused by the combination of too much food and not enough exercise.

One of these children is a fifth-grader named Jessica. In many ways, she is a typical ten-year-old girl who likes movies, music, and fashion. She used to be interested in many other things, too, including her schoolwork and sports. But the weight problem she has struggled with for years has recently gotten worse, and it has taken away much of the fun she once felt doing these activities.

Jessica's height of four feet, six inches is average for a girl her age. But her weight, which has increased dramatically in the past year or so, is now approximately 130 pounds. This means she is **obese**—severely overweight—and her condition is causing many problems for her.

Some of Jessica's problems are medical. Jessica's doctor has told her and her parents that obesity places her at risk of developing a number of very serious medical problems. Jessica already suffers from **asthma**—a serious **respiratory** condition that is made worse by obesity. This condition makes it difficult for her to breathe. She also has trouble sleeping, perhaps because of her breathing problems, and she is often very tired during the day. The doctor is also worried that Jessica may develop a serious, sometimes life-threatening disease called **diabetes**.

If you have asthma, the airways in your lungs may become constricted, making breathing difficult. The medication in an inhaler can help to open them.

Obesity is negatively affecting Jessica's life in many other ways, too. She says that all she wants is to feel normal, but being obese makes this difficult. For example, she used to play soccer at school. But she can no longer play competitively, because she lacks the necessary stamina and her asthma often leaves her too short of breath. Instead of playing, she now watches the games from the sidelines—and, she says, "I don't really feel like doing that anymore."

Something else has recently begun to hurt Jessica deeply. Some of the other children at her school and in her neighborhood have been teasing her about being "fat." Jessica tries not to let their unkind words bother her, but it is not easy. She is well aware that she does not look like many of the other girls she knows—and even less like the thin movie stars and fashion models she sees on magazine covers. She cannot wear the stylish clothes that many girls like, because they are not made in her size. And the sense that she is "different" is making her more and more withdrawn. "I mostly just like to stay home now," she says. "Some days I don't even feel like going to school, because I feel like I don't fit in." Not surprisingly, her grades have begun to suffer.

Many people are trying to help Jessica. A few weeks ago, her parents, both of whom are overweight themselves, began taking her to see a **nutritionist.** The nutritionist is teaching her better eating and exercise habits, which will help her to lead a healthier life and eventually to lose weight. Jessica and her family have begun to eat a more balanced, more nutritious **diet**—more salad, less pizza, is the way her mother describes the change—and to get more exercise, often taking walks together in the evening.

Jessica is also working on feeling better about herself, with the help of a mental health professional called a psychologist. The psychologist is helping her to understand the reasons for her obesity—why she has tended to eat too much of the wrong kinds of foods. "I used to think I ate so much because I was hungry all the time," Jessica says. "But now I know I eat because I get bored, or maybe because something is bothering me." And knowing the reasons for her unhealthy habits helps her to control them.

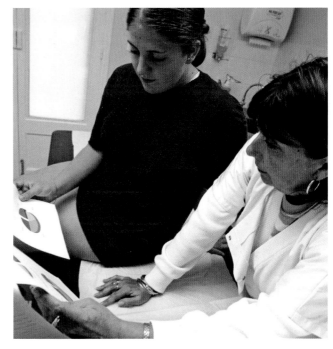

A nutritionist is a trained professional who can help you understand your eating habits and develop a healthier lifestyle.

These changes in the way she lives are beginning to make Jessica feel better, both physically and mentally. She has not really lost any weight yet, but both her nutritionist and her psychologist have told her not to worry about that. The important thing right now is for Jessica to feel better—and she says she does. She is more confident, she has more energy, and she is beginning to do better in school.

With hard work, and a lot of support from family, friends, teachers, and others, Jessica can continue to get healthier. And the millions of other people who suffer from obesity— both children and adults—can learn a valuable lesson from her example.

2

WHAT IS OBESITY?

Obese is a term that doctors, nutritionists, and other healthcare professionals use to describe people who are extremely overweight. This does not simply mean that they are fat, a word that many obesity experts prefer not to use when describing people, or even that they are somewhat **overweight**. People who are obese are so overweight that many normal daily activities are difficult, or even impossible, for them.

An obese child may suffer from respiratory problems, so that he cannot breathe well enough to run, or even walk, comfortably. For another child, obesity may mean that she is not agile or flexible enough to move quickly on the playing field. And many obese children cannot concentrate on their schoolwork, sometimes because their condition keeps them from sleeping well at night.

Obesity can cause many serious medical problems for children, and it can make many other medical conditions worse.

Children who are overweight or obese are far more likely to suffer from asthma than those who are not. Obese children also may get **hypertension**, which can lead to **cardiovascular disease** later in life. Other problems include joint pain, which occurs when a child's still-growing bones must support too much weight, and **sleep apnea**, which makes it difficult to get a good night's sleep.

An obese child is likely to become an obese adolescent, and an obese adolescent is even more likely to become an obese adult. And the health problems faced by obese adults are even more serious than those for children. Obese adults may face life-threatening medical conditions, such as **arthritis**, **cancer**, cardiovascular disease, liver disease, and **stroke**. Some adults actually become so obese—doctors describe these

Doctors blame childhood obesity for the huge increase in diabetes in children—especially a form of the disease called Type 2 diabetes. Type 2 was once so rare in children that it was known as "adult onset" diabetes. But the **Centers for Disease Control and Prevention (CDC)** now estimate that one out of three children born in the year 2000 will develop the disease someday.

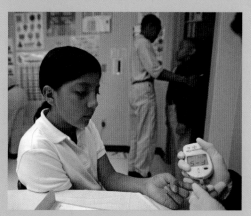

A school nurse checks a young girl's glucose levels to test for diabetes.

A thirty-year study published in the *Annals of Internal Medicine* concluded that nine out of ten men in the United States, and seven out of ten women, will become overweight at some point in their lives.

people as **morbidly obese**—that they are unable to walk or even to stand, and must spend almost all their time in bed.

Health issues are not the only problems confronting people who are overweight or obese. Obese children's inability to take part in games and other physical activities may lead to feeling socially isolated and friendless. Obese children can certainly have many friends, but, unfortunately, this is not always the case. Some children who suffer from obesity are teased, ridiculed, or even bullied by other children. If this mistreatment is allowed to continue, the result may be serious social, emotional, or psychological problems for the obese child. Studies have shown that obese children may suffer from low self-esteem and **depression**, and this may result in their becoming underachievers in school and in other areas of their lives.

The same is true of the obese adult, who often suffers from an even stronger sense of social isolation. Many people believe that the obese are discriminated against, especially in the workplace. Studies have shown that overweight or obese people

Overweight or obese young people may feel left out or rejected, and this sense of isolation may lead to depression.

are less likely to be hired for jobs than are thin people, even when they are equally qualified, and that they are frequently paid less for doing the same jobs.

In recent years, obesity has increased dramatically in many parts of the world, and nowhere is the problem more serious than in the United States. People who are overweight or obese are now the majority in America. Many experts believe that obesity is the most serious health problem facing the country today, and some are now calling it an **epidemic.**

The reasons for the obesity epidemic in the United States are complicated, and we do not yet fully understand them. But many changes in the way we live have certainly contributed to the problem. Americans now get far less exercise than they did in the past, because they are less likely to do manual labor and more likely to drive to work or to school than to walk. We also spend a great deal of our time in **sedentary** activities—watching television, working at computers, or playing video games—that did not even exist a few generations ago.

Another reason for the stunning increase in obesity is the change in our diets. We eat far more than earlier generations did, and the food we eat contains more **fats** and **carbohydrates**—all ingredients that can

The United States has the highest obesity rate of any major country, but a few small countries have even worse rates. Most of them are island nations in the South Pacific, such as tiny Nauru, which has the world's most obese population, with an estimated 94.5 percent of the population either overweight or obese. The reasons for this are unclear, but one may be the fact that some Pacific Island cultures have traditionally viewed physical size as a sign of beauty. The lowest rates of obesity in the world are found in sub-Saharan Africa, which has long suffered from food shortages.

Children who prefer video games to physical activities are much more likely to become overweight or obese.

The packaged snack foods that we often eat while watching television tend to be high in the fats and sugars that are a major cause of obesity.

contribute to weight gain. The foods we eat today also contain fattening man-made ingredients that did not exist in the past, such as **trans fats** and **high-glucose corn syrup**. Trans fats, which are "artificial" liquid fats created by adding hydrogen to solid fats, are widely used in frying and baking, and have been linked to both obesity and heart disease. High-glucose corn syrup is used as a sweetener in everything from soda to snack foods, and adds both more sweetness and more calories than old-fashioned sugar, which is usually made from sugarcane or beets. Some nutritionists also believe that it is processed differently by the body. Instead of using the sweetener for energy, the body tends to store it.

The result of this combination of more-fattening food and less physical exercise is that people gain more weight and are less healthy than ever before. In fact, obesity is so common-place today that it is not simply a problem for the obese person, but also for society as a whole. For example, treatment for obesity-related medical conditions costs government

Young people who compare themselves to celebrities in magazines may end up feeling worse about their bodies and their lives.

agencies and insurance companies billions of dollars every year.

You need only to watch television, look at a magazine, or go to the movies to realize the importance that the modern world places on physical attractiveness. And the people who are considered physically attractive—fashion models and movie stars, for example—are often so thin that most people would find it impossible to look anything like them. Even people who are not obese, or even overweight, feel inadequate because they cannot achieve such unrealistic standards of physical beauty. The pressure to look like these so-called beautiful people can lead to excessive and harmful **dieting**—which seldom leads to permanent weight loss—and even to dangerous **eating disorders**, such as **anorexia nervosa** and **bulimia**. And for people who are obese, the feeling of not measuring up to society's expectations can be overwhelming, and may actually lead them to eat more and become even heavier.

Young people who are obese and feel that society is pressuring them should seek help. They can get the help they need from their families, their friends, and doctors, nutritionists, and other health professionals who can show them how to lead healthier lives. This will almost certainly mean significant changes in their eating habits and in the amount of exercise they get. These lifestyle changes are not easy, and they must continue throughout the person's life. But these changes can result in the individual living a longer, healthier, and happier life.

Experts disagree about who should be considered obese, and even about whether the word should be used at all, especially when describing children and adolescents. Health professionals use a complex set of factors to determine whether someone is obese.

One of the most useful tools used for diagnosing obesity is the **Body Mass Index (BMI)**. This is a number that is determined by comparing a person's weight with his or her height. Experts' opinions about how BMI should be interpreted vary, but the most commonly accepted adult standards used in the United States are the ones developed by the CDC:

- BMI below 18.5: Underweight
- BMI 18.5–24.9: Normal weight
- BMI 25.0–29.0: Overweight
- BMI 30.0 or higher: Obese

People should not assume, based on their BMIs alone, that they are obese, or even overweight. That can be determined only by a health professional—and this is especially true for children and teenagers. Some weight gain is perfectly normal and healthy for growing bodies.

Adults' bodies also come in many different shapes and sizes, so their BMIs vary widely. Many different factors—including age, sex, family medical history, and ethnic origin—can influence how a person's BMI is interpreted. Elderly people, for example, often seem to be underweight according to their BMIs. This is because everyone loses muscle tissue in old age, and muscle weighs much more than fat. The BMI might even suggest that a professional athlete in peak physical condition—with a great deal of relatively heavy muscle tissue—is actually obese, even morbidly so.

For all these reasons, doctors seldom rely on BMI alone

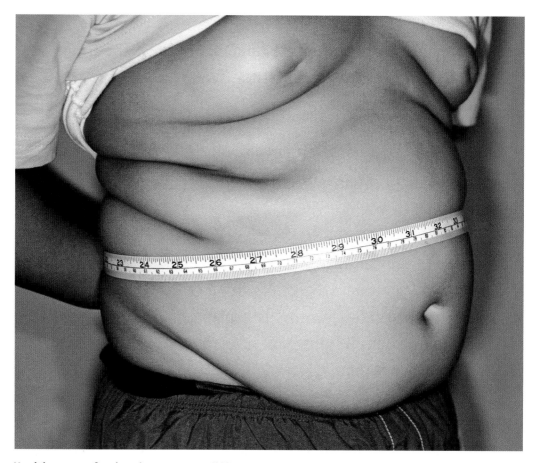

Healthcare professionals use many different methods—including body measurements—to diagnose obesity.

when making a **diagnosis** of obesity. They usually also measure waist size—and sometimes calculate the waist-to-hip ratio. Another technique is to estimate the total amount of fat on a person's body. Some experts believe that the percentage of body fat the person has is a more meaningful indication of obesity than actual body weight. Testing body fat may be done by using instruments called calipers that measure fat by pinch-ing body tissue. Doctors can also measure fat content with devices that send electronic impulses through a person's body. The most accurate method of all, however, is hydrostatic weigh-ing, which is done in a special water tank.

However obesity is defined, there is no question that the number of obese people has increased dramatically in recent years. Between 1960 and 2000, obesity in preschool children (ages two to five years) in the United States more than doubled. For children ages six to eleven, the trend was even worse, with obesity tripling in the same forty-year period. A study by the Institute of Medicine of the National Academies estimates that nine million American children over the age of six are now obese.

People naturally gain weight as they grow older, because the process by which their bodies convert food into energy slows down. This helps to explain why the obesity rate is worst of all for adults. According to the **National Institutes of Health (NIH)** 34.1 percent of all adults in the United States (68.5 million) are overweight, while almost as many (32.2 percent, or 64.7 million) are obese. This means that fewer than half of all American adults are at what doctors consider a healthy weight—and more than half are at risk of contracting the very serious health effects that result from being overweight or obese.

Obesity-Related Conditions

Obesity-Related Conditions in Children

- Asthma and other respiratory problems
- Bone and joint problems
- Depression and other psychological problems
- Diabetes (including Type 2)
- Excessively high levels of cholesterol, **triglycerides**, or **insulin**.
- Hypertension
- Sleep apnea

Additional Obesity-Related Conditions in Adults

- Arthritis (osteoarthritis and rheumatoid arthritis)
- Birth defects (in babies born to obese mothers)
- Cancer (breast, colorectal, endometrial, and esophageal)
- Cardiovascular disease
- Gallbladder disease
- Infertility
- Kidney disease
- Liver disease
- Stroke

Obesity is a major factor in many serious medical conditions.

OBESITY AND HEALTH

Obesity causes, contributes to, or makes worse a huge number of serious health problems. Almost 65 percent of morbidly obese people suffer from hypertension—a condition that can lead to heart disease, stroke, and other potentially fatal health conditions. Obesity can also adversely affect a person's health in some unexpected ways. Someone who is obese may, for example, recover from surgery more slowly than someone who is not. Obese people are also much more likely to suffer from dangerous infections following treatment for wounds or burns.

Some obesity experts believe that every year more than 300,000 deaths in the United States—one out of every eight—are caused by medical conditions directly related to people being overweight or obese. In fact, the federal government considers obesity the second-greatest cause of preventable death in the country today.

THE CAUSES OF OBESITY

The causes of obesity—the reasons some people become obese, while others do not—are far more complicated than was once believed. Research on obesity has changed a great deal in recent years, and it continues to evolve. But there are certain factors that almost all experts agree are crucial:

Different people's bodies store fat in different areas. The abdomen is one of the most common places for fat cells to collect.

The Imbalance Between Diet and Exercise

Our bodies convert the food we eat into energy—usually measured in units called **calories**—through a process known as **metabolism.** When the body takes in more calories as food than it uses as energy, the unused calories are stored as fat cells in a special kind of body tissue, called **adipose tissue.** Adipose tissue tends to be concentrated in certain parts of the body. One of these areas is the abdomen, which is why people often gain weight there. If this imbalance in calories-in/calories-out continues for some time, the person will almost certainly become overweight or obese. And the situation can only get worse as the person gets older, because the metabolism slows down, converting food into energy less efficiently, with age. This is one reason that older people are the group most likely to be obese.

If we are eating more—and there is no question that most of

us are—then we should also be exercising more. Unfortunately, we are actually exercising much less than in the past, and much less than we should be. The United States government recommends that adults get at least thirty minutes of regular, vigorous physical exercise every day, and that children exercise for at least sixty minutes each day. But the NIH estimates that 74 percent of American adults do not engage in such activity. Children are doing somewhat better, but approximately 25 percent of them also do not engage in regular, vigorous physical activity, and a disturbing 14 percent do not get any exercise at all.

The human body uses food-energy in three ways:

• **Thermogenesis**—Approximately 10 percent of food-energy intake is used up in the process of converting the food itself into energy.
• **Basal metabolism**—Another 60 percent of food energy (approximately) is used while our bodies are resting, to maintain basic body functions, such as keeping our body temperature consistent.
• **Physical activity**—The remaining food energy—approximately 30 percent—is used in physical activity.

Heredity

Obesity definitely runs in families. Researchers have identified more than fifty different genes that may contribute to a

Scientists are working hard to identify genes that may contribute to obesity.

tendency toward obesity. A child of obese parents may be twice as likely as other children to become obese. But it is not clear that this is entirely caused by **heredity** (also known as genetics). These children may simply be learning the same habits that made their parents obese: eating too much of the wrong foods and exercising too little.

Friends can have an important influence, too. A research study published in the *New England Journal of Medicine* in 2007 followed more than 12,000 people from the Framingham, Massachusetts, area for thirty-two years. The researchers found that if one person became obese, a friend of that person was 57 percent more likely than the overall population of becoming obese themselves—and a very close friend was an astonishing 171 percent more likely to become obese. Nobody really understands why, but part of the reason may be that having an obese friend makes people more comfortable about being obese—and encourages the behaviors that cause obesity.

Most experts now believe that obesity is usually the result of a combination of behavioral and **genetic** factors. But there are some comparatively rare genetic disorders—such as Bardet-Biedl syndrome, which is related to mental retardation, and Prader-Willi syndrome, which causes almost constant hunger, that are known to cause obesity. Some experts believe that genetics may be responsible for as much as 25 percent of an individual's tendency to become obese.

A study of adopted children suggests that genetics plays a more important role in obesity than researchers once believed. The body-weight patterns of the adopted children were closer to those of their biological parents—whom they had never met—than to their adoptive parents.

Medical Conditions and Treatments

Certain illnesses may cause rapid weight gain, even when a person does not overeat. These include two **hormone** disorders: a rare condition called Cushing's disease and a much more common one known as hypothyroidism. Some medications, such as steroids, which are used to treat many medical conditions, can also cause weight gain. And many **psychiatric** medications used to treat depression, anxiety, and psychosis can also lead to weight gain through increased appetite.

Environmental Factors

Sometimes it is easy to understand why an individual child or adult becomes obese. What is much harder to explain is why so many people, especially in the United States and the rest of the Western world, are becoming obese. To understand why this is happening, we must look at environmental factors—that is, the way we live.

What we eat, and how we eat it, has changed dramatically over the past one hundred years or so. A century ago, most Americans ate smaller meals, ate them at regular times, and mostly ate them at home with their families. Today, the average American eats restaurant or take-out food at least five times a week—and usually uses a car to get it, instead of walking. This is a problem for several reasons. Restaurant portions are much larger than in the past, and commercially prepared foods are usually much higher in fats, carbohydrates, and calories, than food that is prepared at home.

Fast food meals, which are usually packed with fat and calories, are available almost everywhere—even in some school cafeterias.

Fast food, the quick and easy meals that have become so much a part of our daily lives, can be especially dangerous. A typical lunch from a well-known fast-food chain—a quarter-pound cheeseburger, a large order of french fries, and a large soda—totals an incredible 1,380 calories. This is more than half of an active adult's recommended caloric intake for the entire day, which is between 2,000 and 2,500 calories. Moreover, this type of food is usually extremely high in fat (especially **saturated fat**), carbohydrates, and salt (which does not contribute to obesity, but does increase the related risk factor of hypertension).

Snacking on unhealthy foods such as potato chips and soda can easily lead to unwanted weight gain.

People today also eat more, and eat more often, when they are at home. Snacking between meals is far more common than it was in the past, partly because we spend so much more time watching television and doing other sedentary activities. Unfortunately, we often do not realize how much the snack foods we reach for can contribute to obesity. A one-serving size bag of potato chips, for example, may contain 200 calories—one-tenth of the total recommended adult caloric intake for the entire day!

Many of the changes in the way we live today were probably inevitable. Most of us live in places where we cannot simply walk to work or to school. And we are more likely to work in offices than in factories or on farms. So it is not surprising that we get less exercise in our daily lives. The changes in our eating patterns are not surprising either. The stay-at-home mom of the past now probably has a demanding job outside the home, so she has less time to prepare sit-down meals for her family. And most of us are so busy with work and school activities that it is easier to grab a snack as we go out the door than to gather for a family dinner. Unfortunately, when we eat this way, we eat more, and we eat more of the wrong foods. The result of all these changes—however inescapable they may be—is that more people are overweight or obese than at any time in human history.

Environmental factors can influence obesity in some unexpected ways. For example, a study from Britain suggests that poor sleep habits may make children and adults much more likely to become obese. The reason is unclear, but may be related to changes in the way the body metabolizes food. Another possible factor is that people who are tired are less likely to exercise.

3

THE HISTORY OF OBESITY

Obesity is a very modern problem. Throughout most of human history, food was so scarce that most people had to struggle to find enough to eat to avoid hunger, or even starvation. This is still true today in some of the poorest parts of the world, where **malnutrition** remains a very serious problem. It is really only in the past one hundred years or so that many people have had to worry about becoming obese, or even overweight.

Some ancient peoples viewed obesity as something to be admired. Many statues from prehistoric times have been

In the past, obesity was sometimes seen as something to be desired, as this ancient statue seems to show.

found to show women who would be considered morbidly obese today. Nobody knows for certain why these statues were made— they may have been religious objects of some kind—but they seem to show that standards of health and beauty were very different in those times.

It is possible that the scarcity of food in the past may be contributing to the obesity epidemic today. A theory called the **thrifty gene hypothesis** suggests that people who often go hungry develop a genetic tendency to store food as fatty tissue, to be used up during times when food is scarce. Then, in future generations when more food becomes available, their descendants may be more likely to become obese. This may be one of the reasons that obesity is so common in the islands of the South Pacific.

The Pima, a Native American people who have lived in the mountains of Arizona and northern Mexico for thousands of years, may present an example of the thrifty gene at work. Their traditional way of life was one of hard physical work and a low-fat diet. In recent years, however, the Pima of Arizona have adopted a more American diet that is high in fat, and have become more sedentary. They now have one of the highest rates of obesity in the world, and at least half suffer from diabetes, a disease that was once almost unknown among them. But the Pima of Mexico—who have mostly kept their traditional way of life— do not suffer from these problems.

Many ancient peoples did understand that obesity was unhealthy, and tried to find ways to prevent and cure it. The Greek doctor Hippocrates, who lived more than two thousand years ago, observed that overweight people tended to die suddenly. He recommended that they eat less and exercise more. The word *obese* itself, which comes from a Latin root meaning "to eat," shows that the ancient Romans also understood the connection between eating too much and being overweight. Wealthy Romans sometimes tickled their throats with a feather to induce vomiting, so that they could eat more without gaining weight. And some Roman women, like some people with eating disorders today, are said to have starved themselves almost to death to stay thin.

Nonetheless, it was only in the nineteenth century that most people, at least in the Western world, began to have food security—the knowledge that they would usually have enough to eat. And it was only then that obesity started to become more commonplace—and people began looking for ways to control the condition.

Many of the so-called cures for obesity that appeared around this time were useless, and more than a few were actually dangerous. Some were made from harmless and ineffective ingredients such as herbs, berries, and seaweed, but others contained powerful drugs and even poisons, including arsenic and strychnine. In those days, governments did not regulate

Obesity "cures" throughout the ages have promised weight loss using drugs, special diets, and even soaps—like the one offered in this British advertisement from the 1920s.

medications as carefully as they do today, and sellers of obesity treatments were able to make outrageous and often completely false claims about their effects.

During this period, health spas, sanitariums and so-called fat farms where people—mostly the wealthy—could go to be cured of a variety of ills, including obesity, began to spring up. Some

One of the most respected centers for obesity research and treatment in the world is Duke University, in Durham, North Carolina. For decades, Duke's obesity experts have been helping people to lose weight, and training specialists in obesity treatment. Duke now has such a reputation that some obese people who go there for treatment decide to move to Durham, because they think it will be easier to maintain their weight loss if they live in the area.

of these places were legitimate institutions where patients received serious, if not always effective, medical treatment. Others were more questionable places, where patients were given unproven treatments, including **purging** procedures that could actually be quite harmful.

Even as these questionable treatments were becoming widespread, more serious medical and scientific research into obesity was being done. In the 1940s, the Metropolitan Life Insurance Company received a great deal of attention when it published a set of tables showing what were then considered the ideal weights for men and women.

And by the early 1950s, the United States government was already beginning to recognize how serious a problem obesity was becoming, and was trying to find ways to deal with it. These included encouraging more physical exercise and better eating habits, especially among schoolchildren.

Some people tried to find ways to deal with their weight problems on their own. In 1960, several people in Los Angeles began to meet to discuss their weight problems and try to figure out ways to deal with them. They developed a self-help program based on the twelve-step principles of Alcoholics Anonymous. The support group they formed, Overeaters Anonymous, now has an estimated 70,000 members in sixty countries.

America's obsession with weight had become big business by the 1960s. More and more books were published that claimed to be able to help people to lose weight with special diets. Some of their recommendations were sensible, but many advocated highly restrictive diets—for example, eating only cabbage or bananas for days at a time, or taking in only liquids—that were almost impossible to follow for any length of time and could be dangerous. Most people who tried these approaches to weight loss found that they either failed to lose the weight or eventually regained the weight they had lost—and often gained even more. This is frustrating for the person who is overweight or obese, and it can be dangerous, as well. As far back as the 1940s, research suggested that **weight cycling**—repeatedly losing weight, then gaining it all back, and sometimes gaining even more—could be harmful to a person's health. One concern is that this process may strain the heart, making cardiovascular disease more likely.

Today, obesity has become a billion-dollar industry. More and

USDA Food Pyramid

One important development in dealing with America's obesity problem came in 1992, when the United States Department of Agriculture (USDA) introduced its food pyramid. This was a convenient guide that showed the recommended daily servings and portions of the main food groups—bread and other grains, fruits and vegetables, milk products, meat and other foods that are high in **protein**, and fats. In 2005, the USDA replaced it with MyPyramid, a more personalized interactive version that stresses the importance of physical activity much more than the original food pyramid.

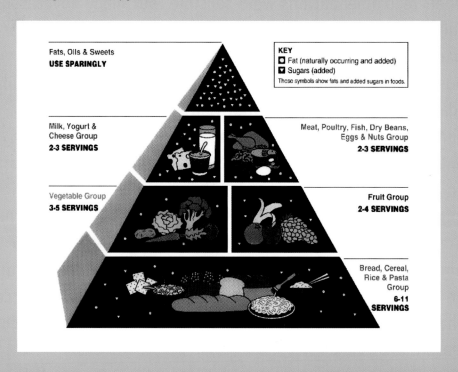

more weight-loss programs
appear every year—in books,
videos, television shows, and
support groups—that promise
to help people lose weight in a
myriad of ways. Weight-loss fads
and fashions change constantly.
For a time, beginning in the
1980s, it was fashionable to
remove almost all dietary fat
from some foods, especially
snack foods. Fat-free cookies and
cakes became very popular, but
the people who ate them did not
realize how the manufacturers
had made up for the absence
of fat. To make their fat-free
products taste good, the
manufacturers increased the

Supermarkets and other food stores now offer
many more choices for people who are trying to
lose weight or simply to eat a healthier diet.

amount of sugar—which made the fat-free foods as fattening
as before, if not more so. More recently, extremely low-
carbohydrate dietary plans, which tell people to eat large
amounts of meat and almost no breads or other foods made
from grains, have become more popular. Most experts now
believe, however, that the key to reducing obesity is not in
removing any particular element from our diets, but rather by

The human body cannot live without fat, but some fats are healthier than others. **Unsaturated fats**, such as those in olive oil and fish, help to maintain healthy **cholesterol** levels. Saturated fats—which are found in whole milk, milk products, and red meat—and trans fats have the opposite effect.

The unsaturated fats in olive oil help a person's body maintain healthy cholesterol levels.

reducing overall caloric intake in a balanced way that people can live with for a lifetime.

Just as was the case in the past, many of today's weight-loss fads are untested, and are sometimes dangerous, as well. One recent example was a drug known as phen-fen, which was a combination of two already available medications. When phen-fen was first introduced in the early 1990s, it showed great promise as a weight-loss medication. Researchers discovered, however, that some people who took it developed serious heart problems, so the Food and Drug Administration (FDA) banned it in 1997. Other treatments that were once fairly common—for example, wiring an obese person's jaws shut to make it impossible to take in any foods except small amounts of liquids—have now mostly been discontinued.

And despite all the diet books and special programs, more and more Americans are becoming more and more obese. The very clear lesson is that dieting simply does not work—especially for people who are seriously overweight or obese. People who diet may lose weight—particularly if they are only slightly overweight and need to lose only a small amount—but they usually regain it, and sometimes more besides. A study by Harvard Medical School researchers in the 1990s found that young people who dieted regularly were actually much more likely to become overweight than those who did not. It is not

More and more weight-loss programs and "diet" books appear every year.

clear why, but one reason may be that dieting changes the body's appetite mechanism, so that people are no longer able to recognize when they are truly hungry and when they are not. Another reason may be that when dieting, people are not targeting the underlying causes, like stress, for poor eating habits. So when stress recurs, people are likely to begin overeating again.

And the trend is spreading across the country, across all age groups, across both sexes, and among very different types of people. One fascinating change in the nature of obesity is that it is no longer restricted mostly to the wealthy, as it largely was in the past. In fact, low-income people are now twice as likely to be obese. There are many reasons for this paradoxical trend. One is that wealthier, better-educated people are generally more aware of good health practices—such as the importance of a balanced diet and exercise—and also have access to better medical advice and treatment. But the reasons certainly go deeper than this.

Many low-income children, for example, live in inner-city neighborhoods where there are few parks and playgrounds and where it may not always be safe to go outside and play. In many inner-city areas, grocery stores that sell healthy foods, such as fresh fruits and vegetables, are often hard to find, but fast-food restaurants serving high-calorie, high-fat foods seem to be everywhere. This may, in fact, be one of the reasons that African Americans and Hispanics—who are more likely than

Children who live in big cities may not have access to many parks because there is not much open space.

Caucasians to live in big cities—are also more likely to become obese. But obesity is certainly not a problem that is limited to cities. Even in rural areas such as Appalachia, where poverty and malnutrition have traditionally caused many people to actually be underweight, people today are becoming obese.

There is no doubt that more people, in the United States and many other parts of the world, are becoming obese—and morbidly obese—than ever before. But advances in scientific research, medical treatment, and public awareness may be giving us the tools we need to help reverse this trend.

4

LIVING WITH OBESITY

Obesity is a serious problem not only for the millions of people who suffer from the condition, but also for society as a whole. The CDC and the World Bank estimate that treatments for overweight and obese people account for somewhere between 9 and 12 percent of all the healthcare spending in the United States. Nearly half of this expense—an amount approaching $100 billion per year—is carried by the federal government, so high rates of obesity mean that we all pay higher taxes. The economic cost of obesity is also carried by businesses. It was estimated as far back as 1994 that businesses lose $3.9 billion every year for obesity-related reasons, such as inability to work because of illness.

The social impact of obesity can be felt in many other ways that are not as easy to express in dollars and cents. Many educators, for example, believe that overweight or obese children underperform in school. And if obese children do poorly in school, they may lack the necessary skills to be successful in

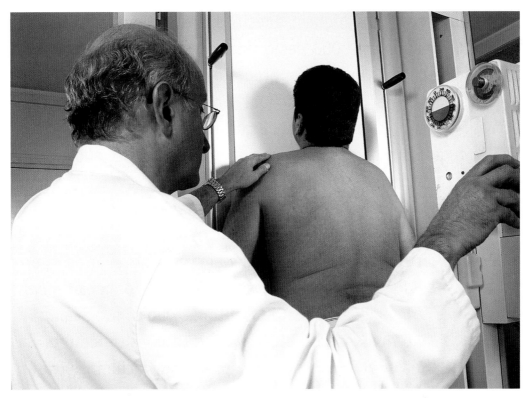

Obesity causes so many health problems that as much as 12 percent of all healthcare spending in the United States may go to obesity-related treatments.

adult life—and American business, then, may lack skilled employees.

These are just some of the reasons that governments, at all levels, are working hard to solve the problem of obesity. In 1999, for example, the U.S. federal government created the Nutrition and Physical Activity Program to Prevent Obesity and Other Chronic Diseases (NPAO), which is now working in twenty-eight states to promote better **nutrition** and exercise habits. Some states have also taken action. The state of Arkansas—

which has one of the highest obesity rates in the country—created a program in 2003 designed to stop the increase of childhood obesity. Among the program's provisions are requirements for healthier foods in school lunches, more physical activity in schools, and more education about health issues. It also requires that schools measure students' BMIs and report them to their parents. This practice is very controversial, because some people believe it could damage a child's self-esteem, but it is becoming more common.

Private citizens and organizations are also focusing on the obesity epidemic. Former president Bill Clinton—who himself has struggled with obesity-related health problems, including heart disease—created the Alliance for a Healthier Generation, a ten-year initiative to help reduce childhood obesity. The Robert Wood Johnson Foundation announced in April 2007 that it plans to spend more than half a billion dollars to work toward the same goal.

Many people and organizations are also working to improve the way society behaves toward people who are overweight or obese.

Obesity is a serious problem in every part of the country, but more so in some areas than others. The states with the highest obesity rates are mostly clustered in the south and the southeast—with Mississippi at the top of the list—while Colorado, Hawaii, and parts of New England have the lowest obesity rates.

Bill Clinton, who struggled with his weight even when he was president, is helping to lead the fight against childhood obesity in the United States.

Experts believe that trans fats in the foods we eat are among the leading causes of obesity—and the FDA estimates that the average American eats 4.7 pounds of these artificial fats every year. In 2006, New York became the first city in the United States to ban trans fats from restaurants. The same year, the Girl Scouts of the USA announced that trans fats had been removed from all of their famous cookies.

The American Obesity Association (AOA) has successfully demanded that governments recognize that obesity is a serious medical condition. This is important because it might lead to insurance companies paying for obesity treatment. The AOA and other organizations—including the National Association to Advance Fat Acceptance (NAAFA)—are working to end discrimination against obese people, especially in the workplace.

DIAGNOSING AND TREATING OBESITY

Doctors, nutritionists, and other experts continue to search for new ways to treat both obesity and the medical conditions related to it. The research in this area is evolving rapidly, and experts' views on the subject have changed greatly.

Nonetheless, at least one thing is clear: Any serious weight-loss program should begin with a visit to the doctor. A general practitioner may refer an obese person to another doctor who specializes in weight-related issues. The doctor will certainly ask for medical history—which should include information

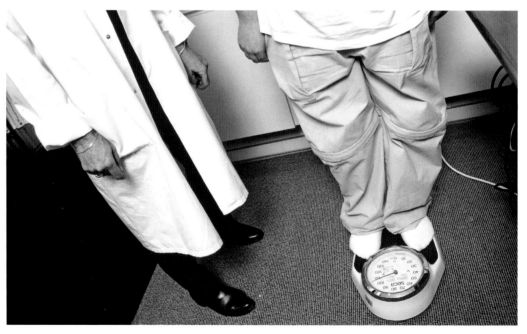

A person planning to start a weight-loss program should always visit the doctor first.

about the patient's family, as well—and will probably request an evaluation from a nutritionist. The nutritionist will try to gain detailed information about the person's dietary habits, often asking the patient to keep a food diary listing everything he or she eats for several days or weeks. Another important part of the evaluation process may be a psychological assessment, to help determine why the patient has become obese—for example, whether the person is overeating due to depression—and what the most effective methods of treatment might be.

At some point in this evaluation process, the patient's BMI will be taken, and his or her body-fat percentage will probably be calculated. The health practitioners involved in the process will try to determine whether the person is in fact obese, and how serious his or her weight problem is. One of the doctor's most important tasks will be to identify any **comorbidities**—cardiovascular disease, for example, or diabetes—which helps determine the correct form of treatment. It will also show the doctor how serious the patient's weight problem is and how well his or her body can tolerate various forms of treatment. The doctor will also want to know about any lifestyle risk factors that may make treatment more difficult, such as smoking and **substance abuse**.

When the diagnosis is complete, the doctor may recommend one or more of the following treatments:

• **Dietary Therapy and Exercise**—Changes in diet—under the direction of qualified medical professionals, such as nutritionists—combined with a carefully designed and supervised exercise program, are essential parts of any obesity treatment.

• **Psychological Counseling**—For many obese people, the most important part of treatment is to understand the causes of the condition. Many people overeat for reasons that have nothing to do with hunger—for example, as a way of making up for unhappiness in their personal lives—and counseling from a qualified therapist may be helpful.

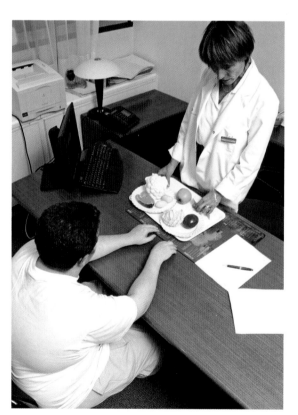

This boy is learning healthier eating habits, with the help of a nutritionist.

• **Medication**—The use of medication to treat obesity is controversial, and researchers are not certain how effective the available medications are. However, some weight-loss medications have been approved by the FDA for use in obesity treatment in the United States. These include orlistat, which partially blocks the body's absorption of fat; phentermine, an appetite suppressant that was one part of

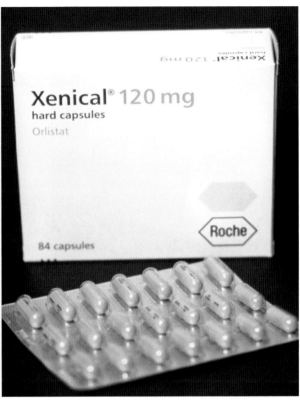

A number of weight loss medications can now be prescribed by a doctor.

the now-banned fen-phen combination; and sibutramine, which sends a signal to the brain to say that a person's **appetite** has been satisfied. In some cases, powerful drugs called amphetamines may be used, as well as certain medications that are normally prescribed for depression and diabetes. Any of these medications can be used only with the approval and under the supervision of a doctor, and it is important to note that most of these medications have not been approved for use by children.

• **Surgery**—If a morbidly obese person has tried many other methods of losing weight, and all methods have failed, a doctor may recommend **bariatric surgery** (sometimes inaccurately called stomach stapling). This is an operation that actually alters the stomach, and sometimes the intestines as well, to limit the amount of food a person can take in and how the body absorbs that food.

Regular physical exercise is one of the most important parts of a healthy lifestyle.

In most cases, some combination of these treatments will work best. Most important is that the patient remembers that treating this condition will require a lifelong commitment. There is no obesity treatment that will work on a short-term basis. The obese person who has decided that it is finally time to deal with the condition must be committed to a lifetime of healthy eating, regular physical exercise, and continuing medical treatment. Support groups with people who have had the same experience can often help the obese person to stay with the treatment in order to lose weight—and to keep it off.

OBESITY PREVENTION

Of course, the best treatment for obesity is not to become obese in the first place. This is actually simpler than it might seem at first. What is required is a combination of a healthy, balanced diet and plenty of physical exercise.

The 2005 recommendations of the FDA's Dietary Guidelines Advisory Committee are an excellent place to start. These recommendations include:

• Taking in a variety of foods from the basic food groups—as defined by MyPyramid—while staying within the individual's energy needs

Eating more fruits and vegetables is an easy way to make your diet healthier.

• Controlling caloric intake to manage body weight
• Being physically active every day
• Increasing daily intake of fruits and vegetables, whole grains, and nonfat or low-fat milk and milk products
• Choosing fats and carbohydrates carefully

These are all very simple steps to take, and they can have a dramatic impact on a person's weight and overall health. The

The best way to lose weight and keep it off is to reduce caloric intake and increase physical activity.

USDA MyPyramid

The new MyPyramid guidelines from the USDA, which were introduced in 2005, take into account many changes in medical research, and in people's lifestyles. Unlike the earlier versions of the food pyramid, MyPyramid recognizes that different people have different nutritional needs. So it provides tools that allow people to design a healthy diet based on many individual factors, including age and sex. MyPyramid gives guidance about how many calories a particular person should eat in a typical day, which food groups those calories should come from, and what serving sizes are healthy. It even gives tips on situations, such as how to make healthy choices when eating in restaurants. Perhaps most important of all, it recognizes that physical exercise is just as vital as a healthy diet, and gives useful recommendations about how to get the exercise we all need. And there is another important change from the old food pyramid: MyPyramid is fun! The USDA hopes that its interactive tools, which include games for children available on the internet, will encourage people to learn more about a healthy lifestyle.

USDA points out that most people could avoid gaining weight simply by reducing their caloric intake by fifty to one hundred calories a day or by getting thirty minutes of physical exercise each day. People who want to lose weight must, of course, reduce their caloric intake by a greater amount and—unless they are unable to do so for medical reasons—get more physical exercise. Anyone who is trying to lose weight, no matter how much or how little, should do so only under the supervision of a doctor or other trained healthcare professional.

What is most interesting about this approach to preventing obesity is that it is not only simple and healthy—it is a pleasure, too! Most people, both children and adults, find that a healthy, active lifestyle is also the most enjoyable lifestyle. And if we all begin to do this, even these very small changes will make an enormous difference for us, for our families, and for society.

GLOSSARY

adipose tissue—A type of tissue in the body where fat is stored.

anorexia nervosa—A life-threatening eating disorder that causes intense fear of weight gain, distorted body image, and dangerous restriction of caloric intake.

appetite—The body's natural desire for food, which makes a person feel hungry.

arthritis—Pain and painful inflammation (swelling) of the joints of the body.

asthma—A respiratory disease that causes wheezing and shortness of breath.

bariatric surgery—Several types of surgery that reduce the capacity of the stomach to limit food intake, and sometimes also to remove part of the intestines to limit food absorption.

basal metabolism—The body's use of food energy to maintain its basic functions.

body mass index (BMI)—A ratio of weight and height that can be used to determine whether a person is overweight or obese.

bulimia—A dangerous eating disorder in which a person overeats and then deliberately vomits, abuses laxatives, or exercises excessively.

calorie—A unit of energy (including, for example, food energy).

cancer—One of a group of diseases that cause unhealthy cells to multiply in the body.

carbohydrates—A substance in food that provides energy for the body to use.

cardiovascular disease—Diseases of the heart and other parts of the circulatory system.

Centers for Disease Control and Prevention (CDC)—The main government agency responsible for improving health conditions in the United States.

cholesterol—A soft, waxy substance found in the blood that may contribute to health problems such as heart disease.

comorbidity—A health condition that occurs at the same time as another health condition in the same body.

depression—A psychological condition that may make a person feel extremely sad or hopeless.

diabetes—A disease in which the body does not produce enough insulin, or the body has trouble recognizing the insulin that it has, causing difficulty breaking down the sugars we eat.

diagnosis—The process by which a doctor identifies a disease or other medical condition.

diet—A person's food intake (what he or she typically eats).

dieting—Eating a special diet (for example, for medical reasons or to lose weight).

eating disorder—A medical problem that causes a person to have unhealthy eating practices.

epidemic—A health problem (such as a disease) that is both widespread and extremely serious.

exercise—Physical movement of the body (for example, through sports).

fat—A substance in food that provides energy.

genetics—The science of heredity.

heredity—The ability of parents to pass on certain characteristics (for example, eye or hair color) to their children.

high-glucose corn syrup—One of a group of chemical products, made from corn, that are often added to foods because of their exceptional sweetness.

hormone—A chemical naturally created by the human body that influences functions such as growth.

hypertension—A medical condition (also known as high blood pressure) that can lead to many other serious health problems.

insulin—A substance in the body that regulates the amount of sugar in the blood.

malnutrition—A serious medical condition caused by eating too little food, or eating food that is too low in nutritional value.

metabolism—The process by which the body converts food into energy.

morbidly obese—Severely or dangerously overweight.

National Institutes of Health (NIH)—A group of U.S. government institutions that conduct medical research.

nutrition—The process by which the human body takes in and uses food.

nutritionist—A healthcare professional trained in the subject of nutrition who studies and treats nutrition-related problems.

obese—Suffering from the medical condition of obesity.

obesity—The condition of being extremely overweight or having an extremely high amount of fat in proportion to the body as a whole.

overweight—Weight that is somewhat more than what is considered normal.

protein—A substance in food that provides energy.

psychiatric—Related to the medical treatment of mental, emotional, or behavioral problems.

purging—Removing food from the body by vomiting, taking laxatives, or exercising excessively.

respiratory—Related to the body's breathing functions.

saturated fat—One of several types of fat that have been shown to have an unhealthy impact on cholesterol levels.

sedentary—Not getting much physical exercise.

sleep apnea—A medical condition that causes breathing to stop repeatedly while a person sleeps, depriving the brain of oxygen and disturbing sleep patterns.

stroke—A serious medical condition that slows or stops blood flow in the brain.

substance abuse—The excessive or otherwise unhealthy use of alcohol, drugs, medications, or other substances.

thermogenesis—The process by which the body converts food into energy.

thrifty gene hypothesis—A theory that people whose ancestors had often gone hungry may develop a genetic tendency toward obesity or other weight-related conditions.

trans fat (or trans-fatty acid)—A synthetic fat, made by adding hydrogen to natural fat, that is sometimes added to food or used in cooking oil.

triglyceride—A common form of fat that, if found in the body in excessively high levels, can contribute to cardiovascular disease.

unsaturated fats—One of a group of fats that have been shown to have a healthy impact on cholesterol levels.

weight cycling (also known as "yo-yo" dieting)—Repeatedly losing and regaining weight.

FIND OUT MORE

Books

Bjorklund, Ruth. *Eating Disorders* (Health Alert). New York: Benchmark Books, 2006.

Edwards, Nicola. *Eating Problems* (Talking About). North Mankato, MN: Chrysalis Children's Books, 2003.

Web Sites

Kidnetic
http://www.kidnetic.com/

KidsHealth for Kids—Staying Healthy
http://www.kidshealth.org/kid/stay_healthy/

MyPyramid—United States Department of Agriculture
http://www.mypyramid.gov

Smart-Mouth—Center for Science in the Public Interest
http://www.cspinet.org/smartmouth/

INDEX

Page numbers for illustrations are in **boldface**

ABOUT THE AUTHOR

Terry Allan Hicks has written books for Marshall Cavendish about everything from the common cold to the Chumash people of California. He lives in Connecticut with his wife, Nancy, and their three sons, Jamie, Jack, and Andrew.